Palinisms

THE ACCIDENTAL
Wit AND *Wisdom*
OF
Sarah Palin

EDITED BY JACOB WEISBERG

A MARINER ORIGINAL
Houghton Mifflin Harcourt
BOSTON   NEW YORK
2010

Copyright © 2010 by Jacob Weisberg

All rights reserved

For information about permission to reproduce
selections from this book, write to Permissions,
Houghton Mifflin Harcourt Publishing Company,
215 Park Avenue South, New York, New York 10003.

www.hmhbooks.com

Book design by Lyndsay Calusine

Library of Congress Cataloging-in-Publication Data
is available.

ISBN 978-0-547-55142-5

Printed in the United States of America

DOC 10 9 8 7 6 5 4 3 2 1

INTRODUCTION

For those used to a diet of oatmeal politics, Sarah Palin is a fiery bowl of moose chili. In a landscape of calculation and careerism, she's a snowmachine roaring across the tundra. In an age of compromise, she stands out as a conviction politician. So far as I can tell, she has four core beliefs:

1. **Things go better with God.**

2. **Yay, Alaska!**

3. **Let's drill that sucker.**

4. **Curse you, political establishment.**

Palinisms occur when Palin expresses one of these views in her idiosyncratically involuted syntax ("It is from Alaska that we send those out to make sure that an eye is being kept on this very powerful nation, Russia"); when she expresses two or more of them in combination ("God's will has to be done, in unifying people and companies to get that gas line built, so pray for that"); or when she says anything at all in her imitable *my sentence went on the Tilt-a-Whirl and got nauseous* way ("And I think more of a concern has been not within the campaign the mistakes that were made, not being able to react to the circumstances that those mistakes created in a real positive and professional and helpful way for John McCain").

But the best Palinisms of all result when the huntress encounters something she wasn't hunting for— that is, when Sarah Palin comes into contact with most anything to do with domestic, foreign, or economic policy. It is this situation that generates those priceless *let me tap-dance and, also, sing for you a little song while you come up with a different question* moments. One such was the juncture in her mind-boggling 2008 interview when Katie Couric asked Palin to name a Supreme Court decision she disagreed with, other than *Roe v. Wade.* Surrounded by hostile forces, out of cartridges for her Remington, she bravely held her ground and kept pulling the trigger:

Palin: Well, let's see. There's — of course in the great history of America there have been rulings, that's never going to be absolute consensus by every American, and there are those issues, again, like *Roe v. Wade,* where I believe are best held on a state level and addressed there. So, you know, going through the history of America, there would be others. But, um.

Couric: Can you think of any?

Palin: Well, I could think of any again that could best be dealt with on a more local level maybe I would take issue with. But, um, you know as a mayor and then as a governor and even as a vice president, if I am so privileged to serve, I would be in a position of changing those things, but in supporting the law of the land as it reads today.

Tina Fey's caricature of Palin as an unprepared high school student trying to bluff her way through an oral exam by mugging and flirting hits its mark not merely because of the genius of the mimicry, but because of its fundamentally accurate diagnosis of Palin as bullshit artist. Palin's exuberant incoherence testifies to an unusually wide gulf between confidence and ability. She is proud of what she doesn't know and contemptuous of those "experts" and "elitists" who are too knowledgeable to be trusted. This curious self-regard echoes through her book, *Going Rogue*, described by the critic Jonathan Raban as "a four-hundred-page paean to virtuous ignorance."

The issue is not that Palin, thrust upon the national stage with little warning, still doesn't know all the details. That's understandable. The issue is that she rarely appears to have the slightest grasp of what she's talking about even when she's supposed to know what she's talking about. For instance, in one of the 2008 campaign's most surreal examples of rhetorical excess, John McCain said Palin "knows more about energy than probably anyone else in the United States of America." A few days later, she offered a sample of her expertise in a town hall meeting: "Oil and coal? Of course, it's a fungible commodity and they don't flag, you know, the molecules, where it's going and where it's not . . . So, I believe that what Congress is going to do, also, is not to allow the export bans to such a degree that it's Americans that get stuck holding the bag without the energy source that is produced here, pumped here."

Bushisms, which I collected for many years, often hinged on a single grammatical or factual error. Palin-isms, by contrast, consist of a unitary stream of patriotic, populist blather. It's like Fox News without the punctuation. It is so devoid of content that it hardly deserves the adjective "truthy." Let's call it "roguey." Palinisms do not have to contain actual evidence of rogue thinking, though; they just have to capture the rogue spirit. It's "Yes, we can, in spite of Them."

The non–Sarah Dittoheads among us have to decide whether to regard this babble — favoring creation science, aerial wolf-shooting, and freedom of the press, so long as the press is "accurate"— as scary or funny. During the 2008 campaign, when there was a real chance that Palin could become the automatic successor to an impulsive, elderly cancer survivor, I found it more scary than funny. After McCain lost, and after Palin terminated her governorship in the effusion of furious gibberish known as her resignation speech, I have found it mostly funny. To be alarmed by Palin today presumes a Republican Party suicidal enough to want her to do more than run its weekend paintball games.

So the spirit of Palinisms is something to be enjoyed.

And we can be sure it's a gift that will keep on giving, for, as she says in her book, "God doesn't drive parked cars." Be warned: The one driving her pickup onto the Fox airwaves and into the Twittersphere is hungry for red meat, hard to reason with, and in a big hurry to get going.

—*Jacob Weisberg*

Palinisms

THE TONYS

"I don't know if I should Buenos Aires or Bonjour, or . . . this is such a melting pot. This is so beautiful. I love this diversity. Yeah. There were a whole bunch of guys named Tony in the photo line, I know that."

— *Addressing a Charity of Hope gathering, Hamilton, Ontario, April 15, 2010*

COP

"I'm not politically correct. I am not one to be a word police."

— *Fox interview with Chris Wallace, February 7, 2010*

GOOD HOCKEY

"It's so good to be here in Michigan, where folks love the good hunting and fishing and the good hockey . . . You're proudly clinging to your guns and religion."

—*Speaking at the Defending the American Dream Summit, Clarkston, Michigan, May 1, 2010*

CONTINENT

"So we discussed what was going on in Africa. And never, ever did I talk about, Well, gee, is it a country or is it a continent, I just don't know about this issue."

—*Fox interview with Greta Van Susteren,
November 11, 2008*

READING

"All of 'em, any of 'em that have been in front of me over all these years."

—*On which newspapers she reads, CBS interview with
Katie Couric, September 30, 2008*

MEDIUMS

"The way that I have understood the world is through education, through books, through mediums that have provided me a lot of perspective on the world."

—*CBS interview with Katie Couric, September 25, 2008*

INTERVIEW I

"Obviously, sometimes I never knew what I was getting into in an interview. Obviously!"

—*Addressing a Charity of Hope gathering, Hamilton, Ontario, April 15, 2010*

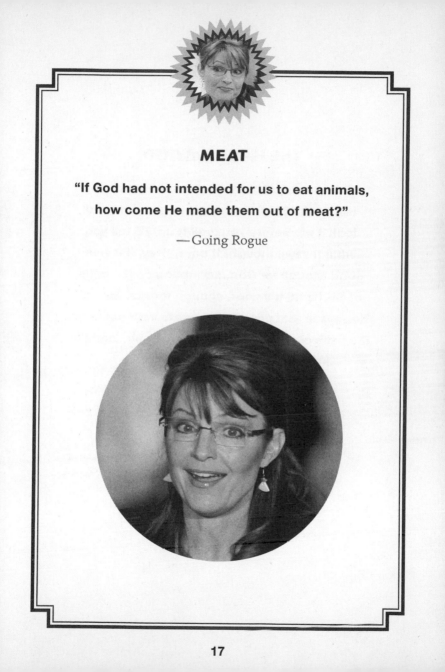

MEAT

"If God had not intended for us to eat animals, how come He made them out of meat?"

—Going Rogue

THE HAND OF GOD

"But then somebody sent me the other day Isaiah 49:16, and you need to go home and look it up. Before you look it up, I'll tell you what it says, though. It says, 'Hey, if it was good enough for God, scribbling on the palm of His hand, it's good enough for me, for us.' He says in that passage, 'I wrote your name on the palm of my hand to remember you,' and I'm like, 'Okay, I'm in good company.'"

—On writing notes on her hand for her Tea Party Convention address, at a speech in Calgary, Alberta, March 6, 2010

CHECKS AND BALANCES

**"I'm the mayor, I can do whatever I want until
the courts tell me I can't."**

*— On spending $50,000 to redecorate the mayor's office
in Wasilla, Alaska, as quoted in* Salon,
September 17, 2008

FRONTIER

"It is from Alaska that we send those out to make sure that an eye is being kept on this very powerful nation, Russia, because they are right there."

—*CBS interview with Katie Couric, September 25, 2008*

FASHION

"I wore my best pair of Carhartts, clogs hand-painted by Alaska artist Romney Dodd, and a T-shirt that said FREEDOM."

—*On how she dressed for the signing of a bill,* Going Rogue

LOVE

"Todd and Christy, this is before they got married, and I remember you guys hooked up at the Alaska State Fair, 'cause Christy, was our, um, she was my nanny when my kids were real little and now my kids are real big."

—Speaking at the Wasilla Assemblies of God church, Wasilla, Alaska, June 8, 2008

PRIVATIZATION

"We took government out of the dairy business and put it back into private-sector hands — where it should be."

—*Resigning as governor, Wasilla, Alaska, July 3, 2009*

UNCLEAR

"I'm very, very pleased to be cleared of any legal wrongdoing . . . any hint of any kind of unethical activity there. Very pleased to be cleared of any of that."

—*On a legislative report asserting that she'd broken the state's ethics law and abused her power in the Trooper-gate scandal, conference call with Alaska reporters, October 12, 2008*

COLOGNE

"With the gray Talkeetna Mountains in the distance and the first light covering of snow about to descend on Pioneer Peak, I breathed in an autumn bouquet that combined everything small-town America with rugged splashes of the Last Frontier."

— Going Rogue

GRIZZLY

"You don't want to deal with moms who are rising up. There in Alaska, I always think of the mama grizzly bears that rise up on their hind legs when somebody's coming to attack their cubs, to do something adverse toward their cubs. No, the mama grizzlies, they rear up, and if you thought pit bulls were tough, you don't want to mess with the mama grizzlies, and I think there are a lot of those in this room."

—Speaking at the Susan B. Anthony List fundraiser, Washington, D.C., May 14, 2010

WORDS

"There's been so many words, Ed, over the state of Alaska, we being the head and not the tail, and, um, I see things now in the works it seems like, things like, that's coming to fruition. Things are perculating!"

—*Speaking at the Wasilla Assemblies of God church, Wasilla, Alaska, June 8, 2008*

ABUNDANTLY

"We built a subcabinet on climate change and took heat from outside special interests for our biologically sound wildlife management for abundance."

—*Resigning as governor, Wasilla, Alaska, July 3, 2009*

GOD

"I can do my job there, in developing our natural resources, and doing things like getting the roads paved, making sure our troopers have their cop cars and their uniforms and their guns, and making sure our public schools are funded. But really, all of that stuff doesn't do any good if the people of Alaska's hearts isn't right with God."

—Speaking at the Wasilla Assemblies of God church, Wasilla, Alaska, June 8, 2008

BIG FOOT

"And I just say bless you. And you guys are just a bunch of cool-looking Christians also. Ben, I don't know you well yet, but looking at you, I bet people are thinking they're going to be interested in Jesus Christ through you because of the way you look: this redheaded Sasquatch for Jesus! You look good!"

—*Speaking at the Wasilla Assemblies of God church, Wasilla, Alaska, June 8, 2008*

POTATOES

"I always remind people from outside our state that there's plenty of room for all Alaska's animals — right next to the mashed potatoes."

—Going Rogue

GOING ON

"There's something going on in Alaska where, you know, we get calls in our office all the time from national media outlets and international media outlets just wondering what's going on in Alaska?"

—*Speaking at the Wasilla Assemblies of God church, Wasilla, Alaska, June 8, 2008*

VEEP I

"Absolutely. Yup, yup."

—*On whether she was ready to be a heartbeat away from the presidency,* People *magazine, August 29, 2008*

VEEP II

"They're in charge of the U.S. Senate, so if they want to, they can really get in there with the senators and make a lot of good policy changes that will make life better for Brandon and his family and his classroom."

—*On the role of the vice president, interview with NBC affiliate KUSA-TV, Denver, Colorado, October 20, 2008*

BLINK

"You can't blink. You have to be wired in a way of being so committed to the mission, the mission that we're on, reform of this country and victory in the war. You can't blink. So I didn't blink."

—On her response when McCain asked her to be his running mate, ABC interview with Charles Gibson, September 11, 2008

ABUSE

"We need to be appreciative of John McCain's call for reform with Fannie Mae, with Freddie Mac, with the mortgage-lenders, too, who were starting to really kind of rear that head of abuse."

—Vice presidential debate, St. Louis, Missouri, October 2, 2008

THE TICKET

"That's exactly what we're going to do in a Palin and McCain administration."

—*Campaign speech, Cedar Rapids, Iowa, September 18, 2008*

VERBAGE

"It was an unfair attack on the verbage that Senator McCain chose to use, because the fundamentals as he was having to explain afterwards, he means our workforce. He means the ingenuity of the American, and of course that is strong, and that is the foundation of our economy. So that was an unfair attack there, again based on verbage that John McCain used."

—*Fox interview with Sean Hannity, September 17, 2008*

ABORT

Palin: Well, let's see. There's—of course in the great history of America there have been rulings that's never going to be absolute consensus by every American, and there are those issues, again, like *Roe v. Wade,* where I believe are best held on a state level and addressed there. So, you know, going through the history of America, there would be others. But, um.

Couric: Can you think of any?

Palin: Well, I would think of any again that could best be dealt with on a more local level maybe I would take issue with. But, um, you know as a mayor and then as a governor and even as a vice president, if I am so privileged to serve, I could be in a position of changing those things, but in supporting the law of the land as it reads today.

—When asked to name a Supreme Court decision she disagreed with (other than Roe), CBS interview with Katie Couric, October 1, 2008

McCAIN

"I can give you examples of things that John McCain has done, that has shown his foresight, his pragmatism, and his leadership abilities. And that is what America needs today."

"I'll try to find you some and I'll bring them to you."

—*Her responses when asked for concrete examples of John McCain's proposals for stricter government oversight of the economy, CBS interview with Katie Couric, September 24, 2008*

FAMILIES

"I know that John McCain will do that and I, as his vice president, families we are blessed with that vote of the American people and are elected to serve and are sworn in on January 20, that will be our top priority is to defend the American people."

—*ABC interview with Charles Gibson,*
September 11, 2008

OBAMA

"If the [media] convince enough voters that that is negative campaigning, for me to call Barack Obama out on his associations, then I don't know what the future of our country would be in terms of First Amendment rights and our ability to ask questions without fear of attacks by the mainstream media."

—*Interview on WMAL-AM radio, Washington, D.C., October 31, 2008*

TODD

"Todd helped as Alaska's first dude with no staff, with no office, being thousands of miles away in a — during a lot of times that with his job in Prudhoe Bay on the North Slope, and commercial fishing. He helped with workforce development issues. Issues that meant a lot to him, and — and people, yes, out there in the real world with Carhartts, and steel-toed boots, and — and hard hats, trying to build this country. Todd helped in that respect."

—*Fox interview with Chris Wallace, February 7, 2010*

TRACK

"Obviously we loved sports, and the baby was born during the spring track season."

—*Explaining her eldest son's name,*
Going Rogue

BRISTOL

"My teenage daughter comes to us, to Todd and me, and she says, 'What's the worst thing you can think of?' And of course, lots of bad things popped into my mind. She was smart to say it that way, because by the time she told us she was pregnant, it was like, oh, okay."

—Addressing a Charity of Hope gathering,
Hamilton, Ontario, April 15, 2010

40

PIPER

"So that evening before the debate, I remember being backstage and looking around for somebody to pray with. And looking around at the campaign staff, and there's nobody to pray with. But backstage there was Piper, at the time my seven-year-old. And I told Piper, I tried to make it easy for her to understand, I said 'Piper, 'kay, I'm going out on stage. I'm debatin' this guy, it's going to be kind of tough.' I said, 'So pray with me, honey.' And I grabbed her hands because that's what we always do, we pray together. I said, 'Piper, just pray that I win.' 'Cause you know, why not?!"

—Addressing a Charity of Hope gathering,
Hamilton, Ontario, April 15, 2010

THE CHILDREN

"Some Alaskans don't mind wasting public dollars and state time. I do. I cannot stand here as your governor and allow millions upon millions of our dollars go to waste just so I can hold the title of governor. And my children won't allow it either."

—Resigning as governor, Wasilla, Alaska, July 3, 2009

GOD'S PLAN

"Pray for our military men and women who are striving to do what is right. Also, for this country, that our leaders, our national leaders, are sending them out on a task that is from God. That's what we have to make sure that we're praying for, that there is a plan and that that plan is God's plan."

—Speaking at the Wasilla Assemblies of God church, Wasilla, Alaska, June 8, 2008

PIPELINE PRAYER

"I can do my part in doing things like working really, really hard to get a natural gas pipeline. Pray about that also. I think God's will has to be done, in unifying people and companies to get that gas line built, so pray for that."

—Speaking at the Wasilla Assemblies of God church, Wasilla, Alaska, June 8, 2008

ENERGY

"Bold visionaries knew this — Alaska would be part of America's great destiny. Our destiny to be reached by responsibly developing our natural resources. This land, blessed with clean air, water, wildlife, minerals, AND oil and gas. It's energy! God gave us energy."

—*Resigning as governor, Wasilla, Alaska, July 3, 2009*

MISTAKES

"And I think more of a concern has been not within the campaign the mistakes that were made, not being able to react to the circumstances that those mistakes created in a real positive and professional and helpful way for John McCain."

—*Fox interview with Bill O'Reilly, November 19, 2009*

OPEN DOOR

"I'm like, okay, God, if there is an open door for me somewhere, this is what I always pray, I'm like, don't let me miss the open door."

—*Fox interview with Greta Van Susteren,*
November 10, 2008

UPSTREAM

"Amidst Hanukkah & Christmas festivities, don't lose sight: 'Trace the universe back 2 God's power & follow His power upstream 2 His wisdom.'"

Quoting Max Lucado, Twitter, @SarahPalinUSA, 7:16 PM Dec 15th, 2009

DOWNSTREAM

"Only dead fish go with the flow."

—*Resigning as governor, Wasilla, Alaska, June 3, 2009*

EVOLUTION

"I didn't believe the theory that human beings — thinking, loving beings — originated from fish that sprouted legs and crawled out of the sea. Or that human beings began as single-celled organisms that developed into monkeys who eventually swung down from the trees."

—Going Rogue

PERCEPTION

"Vietnam, Watergate, the energy crisis, the perception of environmental abuses . . ."

—*Describing the dark period of the 1970s,*
Going Rogue

REALITY

"Oil and coal? Of course, it's a fungible commodity and they don't flag, you know, the molecules, where it's going and where it's not . . . So, I believe that what Congress is going to do, also, is not to allow the export bans to such a degree that it's Americans that get stuck holding the bag without the energy source that is produced here, pumped here. It's got to flow into our domestic markets first."

—*Speaking at a town hall meeting in Grand Rapids,*
Michigan, September 17, 2008

PLUMES

"There are hundreds of trillions more un-
discovered both on shore and offshore, just
piles of energy in that part of North America
that again can be tapped responsibly and
make us all secure."

—*Addressing a Charity of Hope gathering,*
Hamilton, Ontario, April 15, 2010

CONTRIBUTION

"You know, there are man's activities that can
be contributed to the issues that we're dealing
with now, these impacts."

—*CBS interview with Katie Couric, September 30, 2008*

WARM

"A changing environment will affect Alaska more than any other state, because of our location. I'm not one, though, who would attribute it to being man-made."

—*Interview with* Newsmax *magazine, August 29, 2008*

WARMER

"I don't want any Alaskan dissuaded from entering politics after seeing this real 'climate change' that began in August . . . no, we need hardworking, average Americans fighting for what's right! And I will support you because we need you and you can effect change, and I can too, on the outside."

—*Resigning as governor, Wasilla, Alaska, July 3, 2009*

CYNICS

"You are a cynic because show me where I have ever said that there's absolute proof that nothing that man has ever conducted or engaged in has had any effect, or no effect, on climate change."

—*ABC interview with Charles Gibson,*
September 11, 2008

IONS

"Copnhagn Climate Summit;
Obama should boycott in light of
bogus 'findings.' Public leery re:
snake oil science, he must take stand
on Climategate."

Twitter, @SarahPalinUSA, 6:01 PM Dec 7th, 2009

"Glad Wash. Post ran my Op-Ed on 'Global
Warming' Climategate scandal; amazing 2 see
Al Gore's denial of the controversy — it's like
denying gravity."

Twitter, @SarahPalinUSA, 3:59 PM Dec 9th, 2009

"Earth saw clmate chnge 4 ions; will cont 2 c
chnges. R duty 2 responsbly devlop resources 4
humankind/not pollute & destroy; but cant alter
naturl chng."

Twitter, @SarahPalinUSA, 11:57 PM Dec 18th, 2009

CROSSFIRE

"The crossfire is intense, so penetrate through enemy territory by bombing through the press, and use your strong weapons — your Big Guns — to drive to the hole. Shoot with accuracy; aim high and remember it takes blood, sweat, and tears to win."

—*Giving advice to basketball teams, via Facebook, March 28, 2010*

THOSE THINGS

"Ultimately what the bailout does is help those who are concerned about the health-care reform that is needed to help shore up our economy. Helping the — it's got to be all about job creation too, shoring up our economy and putting it back on the right track. So health-care reform and reducing taxes and reining in spending has got to accompany tax reductions. And tax relief for Americans and trade. We've got to see trade as opportunity, not as a competitive, scary thing. But one in five jobs being created in the trade sector today. We've got to look at that as more opportunity. All those things."

—*CBS interview with Katie Couric, September 25, 2008*

SPENDING

"When Washington passed a $787 billion stimulus bill, we were nervous because they just spent $700 billion to bail out Wall Street. On the state level, as a governor, we knew a lot of that money came with fat strings attached. The federal government was going to have more control over our states. They were going to disrespect the Tenth Amendment of our Constitution by essentially bribing with us."

—*Speaking at the Tea Party Convention, Nashville, Tennessee, February 6, 2010*

JOBS

"One state even spent a million bucks to put up signs that advertised they were spending the federal stimulus projects or, as someone put it, this was a $1 million effort to tell you it is spending your money. And it didn't create a single job."

—*Speaking at the Tea Party Convention, Nashville, Tennessee, February 6, 2010*

PORK

"Representative Don Young especially,
God bless him, with transportation — Alaska
did so well under the very basic provisions
of the transportation act that he wrote just
a couple of years ago. We had a nice bump
there. We're very, very fortunate to receive
the largesse that Don Young was able to
put together for Alaska."

—*Alaska Professional Design Council candidate forum,*
Anchorage, Alaska, September 27, 2006

THE BRIDGE

"We need to come to the defense of Southeast Alaska when proposals are on the table like the bridge and not allow the spinmeisters to turn this project or any other into something that's so negative."

— On the "Bridge to Nowhere," interview with
Ketchikan Daily News, *October 2, 2006*

"I told the Congress thanks but no thanks on that 'Bridge to Nowhere.' If our state wanted a bridge, we'd build it ourselves."

— Campaign speech, Albuquerque, New Mexico,
September 6, 2008

AIRSPACE

"As Putin rears his head and comes into the airspace of the United States of America, where — where do they go? It's Alaska. It's just right over the border."

—On her foreign policy experience, CBS interview with Katie Couric, September 25, 2008

NEIGHBORS I

"Our, our next-door neighbors are foreign countries, there in the state that I am the executive of."

—CBS interview with Katie Couric, September 25, 2008

I SPY

"They're our next-door neighbors, and you can actually see Russia from land here in Alaska, from an island in Alaska."

—On her foreign policy expertise, ABC interview with Charles Gibson, September 11, 2008

BORDERS

"That Alaska has a very narrow maritime border between a foreign country, Russia, and, on our other side, the land boundary that we have with Canada. It's funny that a comment like that was kinda made to . . . I don't know, you know . . . reporters."

—On how being near Russia gives her foreign policy experience, CBS interview with Katie Couric, September 25, 2008

DINGY

"You know how many people ask me on the campaign trail if I was Canadian? They think that we talk alike. We say 'eh' too, in Alaska. Never thought anything of it until some reporters . . . I'm the dingy one and they're asking me if I'm Canadian as I'm running for VP. These reporters, because of the way that I talk."

—*Addressing a Charity of Hope gathering, Hamilton, Ontario, April 15, 2010*

DICTATORS

"My concern has been the atrocities there in Darfur. And the relevance to me with that issue, as we spoke about Africa and some of the countries there that were — kind of the people succumbing to the dictators and the corruption of some collapsed governments on the continent."

—Fox interview with Greta Van Susteren,
November 11, 2008

THE BAD GUYS

"It is obvious to me who the good guys are in this one and who the bad guys are. The bad guys are the ones who say Israel is a stinking corpse and should be wiped off the face of the earth. That's not a good guy who is saying that. Now, one who would seek to protect the good guys in this, the leaders of Israel and her friends, her allies, including the United States, in my world, those are the good guys."

—CBS interview with Katie Couric, September 25, 2008

BOMB IRAN

"Okay, we're confident that we're going to win on Tuesday, so from there, the first one hundred days, how are we going to kick in the plan that will get this economy back on the right track and really shore up the strategies that we need over in Iraq and Iran to win these wars?"

— *Fox interview with Greta Van Susteren, October 31, 2008*

NEIGHBORS II

"They are also building schools for the Afghan children so that there is hope and opportunity in our neighboring country of Afghanistan."

— *Speaking at a fundraiser in San Francisco, October 5, 2008*

TROOPS

"So the things that he has done right now as president in protecting the country, more power to him. We appreciate that he kind of went there fully with the commanders on the ground, asking for more reinforcements in Afghanistan. Couldn't get there all the way with these guys, but kind of went there. Good, more power to you."

—*Fox interview with Chris Wallace, February 7, 2010*

MISUNDERESTIMATED

"When you come into a position underestimated it gives you an opportunity to prove the pundits and the critics wrong."

—*Talking with an impostor who she believed was the French president, Nicolas Sarkozy, AP, November 1, 2008*

NO COMMENT

"We get back to the who, what, where, when, and why, and allow the viewers and the listeners and the readers to make up their own minds and not so much commentary, I think, being involved in mainstream media's questioning and reporting on candidates."

—*Post-election interview on* Larry King Live, *November 12, 2008*

MAKING IT UP

"Together we stand with gratitude for the troops who protect all our cherished freedoms. This includes our First Amendment guaranteed freedom of speech — which, par for the course — I shall exercise. First, with some 'straight talk,' I will address some, just some, in the media because another right that is protected is the freedom of the press. You have such important jobs reporting facts and informing the electorate and exerting power to influence. You represent what could and should be a respected and honest profession that could and should be a cornerstone of our democracy. Democracy depends on you. That is why our troops are willing to die for you. So, how about in honor of the American soldier you quit making things up."

—*Farewell address, Fairbanks, Alaska, July 26, 2009*

BACK TO WORK

"I love my job as governor. There is a tremen-
dous amount of work to do in Alaska as we
develop our resources and contribute more
to the United States of America, to allow us to
be secure and prosperous. Look forward to
continuing doing my duties as governor."

—*Post-election interview* on Larry King Live,
November 12, 2008

QUITTERS

"It may be tempting and more comfortable to just keep your head down, plod along, and appease those who demand 'Sit down and shut up,' but that's the worthless, easy path; that's a quitter's way out."

—*Resigning as governor, Wasilla, Alaska, July 3, 2009*

EXPLANATION

"How sad that Washington and the media will never understand; it's about country."

—Resigning as governor, Wasilla, Alaska, July 3, 2009

FEDERAL

"I think on a national level your Department of Law there in the White House would look at some of the things that we've been charged with and automatically throw them out."

—On how a nonexistent department would save her from charges of unethical behavior, ABC interview with Kate Snow, July 7, 2009

STATE

"We don't have to feel that we must beg an allowance from Washington — except to beg the allowance to be self-determined."

—*Farewell address, Fairbanks, Alaska, July 26, 2009*

IRONY

"Believe it or not — this was in the '60s — we used to hustle on over the border for health care that we would receive in Whitehorse. I remember my brother, he burned his ankle in some little kid accident thing and my parents had to put him on a train and rush him over to Whitehorse, and I think, isn't that kind of ironic now. Zooming over the border, getting health care from Canada."

—*Speech in Calgary, Alberta, March 6, 2010*

ARROGANCE

"Copenhgen=arrogance of man 2 think we can change nature's ways. MUST b good stewards of God's earth, but arrogant & naive 2 say man overpwers nature."

Twitter, @SarahPalinUSA, 11:44 PM Dec 18th, 2009

BABY

"And while we're at it, let's expedite the regulatory and permitting and legal processes for on and offshore drilling."

—*Speaking at the Tea Party Convention, six weeks before the BP oil spill, Nashville, Tennessee, February 6, 2010*

SCREW IT

"I have the honor to speak with you for a bit before I get to introduce you to Michael Reagan. And what I'm going to do in introducing Michael is to continue to encourage him, to continue to be bold and to call it like he sees it, and to screw the political correctness that some would expect him to have to adhere."

—*Introducing Michael Reagan at a speech on the fifth anniversary of his father's death, Anchorage, Alaska, June 3, 2009*

BIRTHERS

"I think the public rightfully is still making it an issue. I think it's a fair question."

—*On whether she would make an issue of President Obama's birth certificate. Interview with syndicated radio host Rusty Humphries, December 3, 2009*

HOPE

"We have real hope now to turn around what it is that President Obama warned us he would do to America."

—*Promoting the congressional candidate Vaughan Ward, Boise, Idaho, May 21, 2010*

THE MESSIAH

"When the American people elected President Obama, they gave him responsibility to handle this disaster. He promised to 'heal the earth, and watch the waters recede . . .' or something far-fetched like that."

—*On the BP oil spill, Facebook note posted May 27, 2010*

THE BULLY PULPIT

"I'm sick and tired of hearing about Obama and the White House coming out with yet another crisis."

—*On* The Sean Hannity Show, *April 27, 2010*

HEARTS VERSUS MINDS

"Ronald Reagan spoke to us then, and with us. Here in our hearts is where he reached us, and that's where he won the arguments."

—*Introducing Michael Reagan, Anchorage, Alaska, June 3, 2009*

KERRY

"What a loon, I thought. What an elitist loon."

—*On John Kerry,* Going Rogue

RAND

"A bit of a libertarian, but, you know, heaven forbid that we go the opposite direction of a libertarian and what they are believing in."

—*Concerning Rand Paul, on* The Sean Hannity Show, *May 18, 2010*

SMALL TOWNS

"We believe that the best of America is not all in Washington, D.C. . . . We believe that the best of America is in these small towns that we get to visit, and in these wonderful little pockets of what I call the real America, being here with all of you hardworking, very patriotic, um, very, um, pro-America areas of this great nation."

—*Campaign fundraiser, Greensboro, North Carolina, October 16, 2008*

ROCK ON

"On bus 4 ride North=book event in Sandpoint; stop in Idaho snow-machine shop owned by Todd's Iron Dog buddies; small biz owners rock r economy!"

Twitter, @SarahPalinUSA, 4:21 PM Dec 10th, 2009

VIOLATION

"The perversion over these last years of what the media has done to conservatives, I think it's appalling and it violates our freedom of the press."

—*Promoting the congressional candidate Vaughan Ward, Boise, Idaho, May 21, 2010*

TRUTH

"One thing we can all agree on, though, is how much we respect and want to protect the freedom of the press and we have that in common, so at the end of the day, I think as long as we're protecting that and not abusing the right — we have to be writing truth — then we'll get along just fine tonight."

—*Speaking at the TIME 100 gala, New York City, May 4, 2010*

COLLUSION

"Let me ask you, why is it, considering how fast the world is spinning, and world-changing events that go on all over the globe that affect our lives, world-changing events, thousands of them every day, why do you suppose that the same big three, supposedly competing networks, that have virtually the same news content every night?"

—-*Introducing Michael Reagan, Anchorage, Alaska, June 3, 2009*

THE FOURTH BRANCH

"I would like to kind of help build back that credibility in that cornerstone of our democracy called our media, allowing for the checks and balances that government needs."

—*Post-election interview on* Larry King Live, *November 12, 2008*

COVERING

"I think that it would be absurd to not consider what it is that I can potentially do to help our country. I don't know if it's going to be ever seeking a title, though. It may be just doing a darn good job as a reporter or covering some of the current events."

—*On whether she'll run for office in 2012, Fox interview with Chris Wallace, February 7, 2010*

PLATFORM

"You know, this is not about me. But I do appreciate the platform that I've been given."

—*On Fox News Sunday, May 23, 2010*

FEMINISM

"For far too long when people heard the word feminist they thought of the faculty lounge at some East Coast women's college, right. And no offense to them, they, they have their opinions and their voice, and God bless 'em, they're just great."

—*Speaking at the Susan B. Anthony List fundraiser, May 14, 2010*

NOT THERE

"And obviously me not being, heck, not many of us here tonight are in that political, financial, academic, elite center of power. We're not there."

—*Introducing Michael Reagan, Anchorage, Alaska, June 3, 2009*

QUALIFICATIONS

"I want to encourage people who don't have any elected office experience, not some kind of fat elite résumé in their back pocket."

—*On who should run for office, speaking at the Tea Party Convention, Nashville, Tennessee, February 6, 2010*

CONTROL

"Friends, we need to be aware of the creation of a fearful population, and fearful lawmakers being led to believe, that Big Government is the answer to bail out the private sector because then government gets to get in there and control it, and — mark my words — this is going to happen next, I fear — bail out next debt-ridden states. Then government gets to get in there and control the people."

—*Introducing Michael Reagan, Anchorage, Alaska, June 3, 2009*

TEA TIME

"We're living proof that you don't need an office or a title to make a difference, and you don't need a proclaimed leader as if we are all just a bunch of sheep and we're looking for a leader to progress this movement."

—*Speaking at the Tea Party Convention, Nashville, Tennessee, February 6, 2010*

SIGNS

"It's been clever too being a part of these Tea Party rallies, seeing some of the signs in the audience, and some your signs today too. You can learn a lot about what the sentiment is out there in the American public just by reading the signs in some of these movements."

—*Speaking at the Susan B. Anthony List fundraiser, May 14, 2010*

POSTERS

"Usually, if there's a bad poster out there, I pretend I don't even see it; but yesterday I could not miss it; they were these life-size pictures of naked people. I was like, okay."

—*Addressing a Charity of Hope gathering, Hamilton, Ontario, April 15, 2010*

HYPOTHETICALS

"He wanted to talk about, evidently, some hypotheticals as it applies to impacts on the Civil Rights Act, as it impacts our Constitution."

—*Defending Rand Paul, on Fox News Sunday, May 23, 2010*

ARTICULATE

"Candidates running as common-sense constitutional conservatives have to prove that we have very articulate alternatives to what's going on with the policy proposals in Washington."

—*Speaking at the Defending the American Dream Summit, Clarkston, Michigan, May 1, 2010*

INTERVIEW II

"I'm sitting here talking to Chris Wallace today."

—*On how she knew that her opponents didn't win, Fox interview with Chris Wallace, February 7, 2010*

HECK

"The hecklers are funnier than heck."

—*Addressing a Charity of Hope gathering, Hamilton,
Ontario, April 15, 2010*

REDNECK

**"I'm Googling the latest redneck jokes,
because I had to do a speech where a guy
who's kind of famous for redneck jokes was
going to introduce me, so I wanted to one-up
him . . . Anyway, I'm Googling these jokes trying to find something funny to one-up this guy,
and all these jokes I'm Googling on rednecks,
I'm thinking, that's not funny, that's me!"**

—*Promoting the congressional candidate Vaughan
Ward, Boise, Idaho, May 21, 2010*

ADVANCING

"In the words of General MacArthur said, 'We are not retreating. We are advancing in another direction.'"

—*Resigning as governor, Wasilla, Alaska, July 3, 2009*

FINAL WORDS

**"Nuclear weaponry, of course, would be the
be-all, end-all of just too many people in too
many parts of our planet."**

—*CBS interview with Katie Couric, September 25, 2008*

POSTSCRIPT

**"I didn't really had a good answer,
as so often — is me."**

—*On writing notes on her hand for her Tea Party
Convention address, at a speech in Calgary, Alberta,
March 6, 2010*

BONUS!

top ten tweets
of 2010
@SarahPalinUSA

---

1. **"U kidding, Empire State Bldg officials?
   U won't honor Mother Theresa's
   compassionate, selfless efforts for
   humanity, but honor Communist Mao?"**
   9:44 AM Jun 10th

---

2. **"Extreme Enviros: Drill, Baby,
   Drill in ANWR — Now Do You Get It?
   http://fb.mezWxkjbw8."**
   3:17 PM Jun 2nd

---

3. **"Research is your friend, News Media.
   Try it sometime. http://fb.me/y1SvObvs."**
   11:39 AM May 15th

---

4. "Unbelievable, Outrageous. 'Whether we like it or not, we remain a dominant military superpower' — Obama YES, Mr. Pres, we LIKE knowing we r strong."

6:15 AM Apr 15th

---

5. "Sean Hannity docu tonight! It captures essence of T-Party movement, which is U.S. political future bc we crave freedom & opportunity & common sense."

3:11 PM Feb 23rd

---

6. "Brought to Pelosi's attention that her Obamacare 'process' is unconstitutional, she replies: 'But I like it.' This takes America's breath away."

10:36 AM Mar 16th

---

7. "Happy B'day, Glenn Beck! Ah, the wisdom of our elders . . ."

9:41 AM Feb 10th

---

8. **"Man-made Global Warming=Snow Job. More scientific shake-up today reveals more bunk, making public doubt data. See http://tinyurl.com/y9gsnny."**

12:23 AM Feb 19th

9. **"Good, hardworking pro-business Union MEMBERS should oppose their Union BOSSES backroom deal on this; unfortnately/unfairly paints all of'm bad."**

7:10 AM Jan 15th

10. **"Commonsense Conservatives & lovers of America: 'Don't Retreat, Instead— RELOAD!' Pls see my Facebook page."**

9:31 AM Mar 23rd

Photo Credits

J. Scott Applewhite/AP Photo: 20, 54, 75

Robyn Beck/Getty Images: 33, 87

Al Behrman/AP Photo: 17, 28, 45, 51, 71, 77, 93

Joe Burbank/AP Photo: 56

Charlotte Observer/MCT/Landov: 40, 85

Chicago Tribune/MCT/Landov: 14, 68

Ron Edmonds/AP Photo: 46, 52, 61, 84, 91

Morry Gash/AP Photo: 32, 89

Charles Krupa/AP Photo: 55, 82

MAI/Landov: 62

Tom Miller/AP Photo/Ketchikan Daily News: photo
in burst at page tops, 2, 19, 76, 90

Clark James Mishler/Getty Images: 37, 67

Ed Reinke/AP Photo: 50

Orlando Sentinel/MCT/Landov: 24, 27, 71, 72, 91

Steve Pope/Landov: 36, 60

Reuters/Landov: 11, 22, 34, 42, 80, 92

Paul J. Richards/Getty Images: 21, 38, 65, 79